ROUTE 66

TRAVEL GUIDE 2024

The Ultimate Handbook for First-Time Travelers to an Unforgettable Historical Odyssey

Discover Its History, Cultural Influence, Directions, Best Places, Tips, and More

Charlie Hamlin

Disclaimer

Copyright © by Charlie Hamlin 2024
All rights reserved.

Before this report is copied or imitated in any way, the publisher's assent should be acquired. In this manner, the items inside can neither be put away electronically, moved, nor kept in a data set. Neither To a limited extent nor full might the report at any point be replicated, filtered, faxed, or held without endorsement from the publisher.

Table Of Contents

Map of Route 66, Los Angeles
Introduction
Chapter 1: Overview of Route 66
    Historical and Modern Significance
    The Culture Surrounding Route 66
    Stories of People Who Shaped Route 66
        Cyrus Avery - The Visionary Trailblazer
        John T. Woodruff - The Heartland Advocate
        Angel Delgadillo - The Guardian Angel of the Iconic Route 66
        Bobby Troup - The Melodic Voyager
        Jack D. Rittenhouse - The Highway Chronicler
    Landscapes and Geographical Features of Route 66 by Region
    Languages Spoken in Regions and Communities Along the Route
    Useful Slangs and Phrases for First-time Travelers On Route 66
Chapter 2: Preparing for the Route 66 Adventure
    When to Cruise Route 66
    Choosing the Right Vehicle
    Budgeting and Costs
    What to Pack
    Fuel and Service Costs
    Environmental Considerations
    Road Conditions and Weather Challenges
Chapter 3: Navigating Route 66

Starting Points
- Chicago, Illinois (Eastern Starting Point)
- Santa Monica, California (Western Terminus)

Ending Points
- Santa Monica, California (Eastern Starting Point)
- Chicago, Illinois (Western Terminus)

Chapter 4: Regional Food and Drink Options Along Route 66

Chapter 5: Accommodation Options

Chapter 6: Outdoor and Recreational Activities

Chapter 7: Sightseeing

Side Trips from Route 66
- Taos Pueblo - New Mexico
- Hoover Dam - Nevada/Arizona Border
- Acoma Pueblo - New Mexico
- Grand Canyon National Park, Arizona
- Meteor Crater, Arizona
- Petrified Forest National Park, Arizona
- Carlsbad Caverns National Park, New Mexico

Monuments and Memorials Along the Route

Museums and Galleries Along the Route

Roadside Americanas

Recommended itinerary for first time Tourists

Festivals and Events

Nightlife and Entertainment

Memorabilia and Souvenirs

Chapter 8: Exploring Some Top Cities Along Route 66

Overview of Chicago with Map

Overview of St. Louis with Map

- Overview of Oklahoma City with Map
- Overview of Santa Fe with Map
- Overview of Los Angeles with Map
- Overview of California with Map

Chapter 9: Health and Safety Precautions
- Vehicle Maintenance
- Staying Safe
- Emergency services

Conclusion

Map of Route 66, Los Angeles

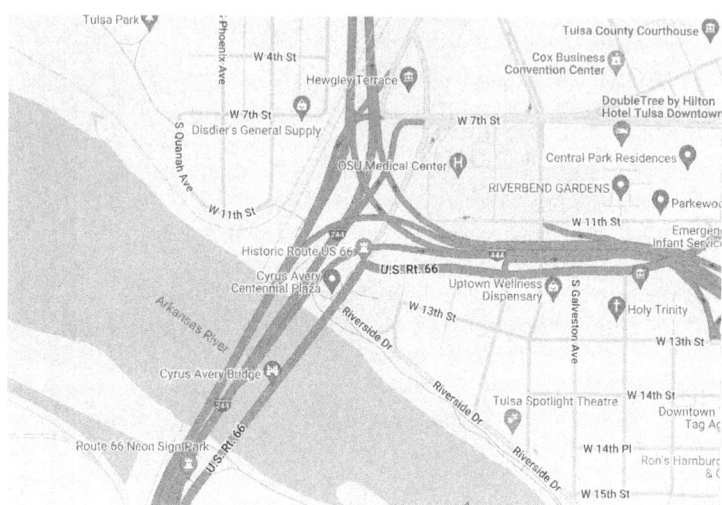

Introduction

In the vast expanse of America's heartland, where the amber waves of grain meet the boundless skies, a journey of self-discovery unfolds on the storied blacktop of Route 66. "Route 66 Travel Guide" beckons readers into the nostalgic embrace of the open road, weaving a tapestry of adventure, history, and personal transformation.

Meet Jack Thompson, a soul-searching wanderer haunted by the monotony of urban life. The guide follows Jack's tire tracks as he embarks on a transformative expedition along the legendary Route 66, carrying a tattered map and fueled by the whispers of the highway's lore. Each mile unravels layers of the past, connecting him to the soul-stirring tales that echo through time.

As Jack cruises through the heartlands of America, readers are transported to iconic landmarks like the Gateway Arch in St. Louis and the sun-kissed streets of Santa Monica. Alongside historical insights, the guide delves into the personal odyssey of Jack, as he befriends fellow travelers in roadside diners and embraces the haunting beauty of ghost towns left frozen in time.

Chapters unfold like a series of postcards from the road, capturing the neon-lit nostalgia of classic motels, the savory aroma of roadside diners, and the vibrant culture of towns that refuse to fade away. From the enigmatic allure of the Grand Canyon to the kitschy charm of the Wigwam Motel, Jack discovers the heartbeat of Route 66.

"Route 66 Travel Guide" transcends the conventional travel guide, inviting readers to explore the highway not merely as a route but as a pilgrimage. Jack's encounters with locals, artists, and dreamers shape the narrative, demonstrating that the magic of Route 66 lies not just in its asphalt but in the stories etched on its surface.

In the end, "Route 66 Travel Guide" is an ode to the American spirit – resilient, diverse, and forever on the move. Through Jack's lens, readers will not only learn about the attractions that dot the iconic highway but also find inspiration to embark on their own personal odyssey, discovering that the Mother

Road is more than just a route; it's a metaphor for life's journey, where each turn holds the promise of adventure and self-discovery.

11

Chapter 1: Overview of Route 66

Historical and Modern Significance

Route 66, often referred to as the Mother Road, holds profound historical significance in the American narrative. Established in 1926, this iconic highway originated during a transformative period in the United States marked by a surge in automobile ownership and a pressing need for improved road infrastructure. Stretching 2,448 miles from Chicago, Illinois, to Santa Monica, California, and traversing eight states, Route 66 became one of the original U.S. highways, embodying the spirit of freedom and adventure.

During the 1930s and 1940s, Route 66 played a crucial role as a lifeline for travelers and migrants seeking refuge from the challenges of the Dust Bowl and the Great Depression. The highway provided a path to hope and opportunity, connecting communities and facilitating the movement of people in search of a better life. Additionally, Route 66 served a strategic purpose during World War II, functioning as a vital route for military transport.

However, the highway gradually lost its prominence with the introduction of the Interstate Highway System in the 1950s, leading to its official decommissioning in 1985. Despite this, Route 66's historical legacy lives on in popular culture through literature, music, and film, encapsulating the essence of a bygone era and preserving a unique chapter in American history.

Modern Significance:

In the modern era, Route 66 continues to play a significant role, albeit in a different context. Designated as a National Scenic Byway and Historic Route 66, the highway has become a cherished destination for travelers seeking a nostalgic journey through America's past. Tourists and road-trip enthusiasts embark on the route to experience the charm of vintage Americana, exploring well-preserved or restored landmarks, including classic motels, diners, and roadside attractions.

The modern significance of Route 66 is also evident in its role as a symbol of community resilience and economic revitalization. Many towns along the route have embraced their historical connection to Route 66, establishing museums, festivals, and events that celebrate the heritage of the highway. This engagement with the past fosters a sense of community identity and provides economic opportunities for local businesses, contributing to the overall vitality of these regions.

Moreover, Route 66 remains relevant in popular culture, with literature, music, and film continuing to celebrate its mystique. The highway has become an iconic backdrop for artistic expressions that capture the enduring spirit of freedom, adventure, and the open road. Through these various dimensions, Route 66 maintains its modern-day significance as a living testament to America's history, a cultural icon, and a source of inspiration for those who seek to explore the heart of the country's heritage.

The Culture Surrounding Route 66

Like the road itself, the culture around Route 66 is rich in history and diversity. The highway became a melting pot of cultures, customs, and experiences as it passed through numerous states and geographical settings. Route 66 has had a profound impact on American society, influencing everything from the thriving metropolises of Chicago and Los Angeles to the sleepy little towns and rural villages that line its path.

The connection of Route 66 to the American road trip is among its most enduring cultural legacies. The highway has come to represent exploration and adventure because of its winding route across the American heartland. Route 66's broad road and the promise of discovery it offers have inspired countless travelers, artists, writers, and performers.

The rich cultural tapestry of the route has also been enhanced by the diversity of its communities. Route 66 has served as a conduit for the flow of ideas, customs, and artistic expression in a variety of contexts, from the dynamic jazz clubs of St. Louis to the Native American history in New Mexico. The folk art, music, food, and local festivals that have blossomed along the highway's length are evidence of its effect.

Another thing that has spurred entrepreneurship and innovation is Route 66. Mid-century America was characterized by an innovative and optimistic spirit, which was mirrored in the businesses that sprung up along the highway, including diners, motels, gas stations, and tourist attractions. In an effort to draw tourists, several of these businesses used striking, eye-catching designs and marketing techniques, which resulted in the creation of a unique look that has come to be associated with Route 66.

Apart from its influence on American society, Route 66 has captivated the interest of individuals globally. The highway has become famous as a result of its representation in literature, movies, and music, luring tourists from all over the world who want to experience its charm and history for themselves.

Through cultural events, museums devoted to its legacy, and preservation initiatives, Route 66 is still remembered today. The road's lasting appeal as a representation of liberty, self-reliance, and the American ideal guarantees that its cultural significance will last for many more years. Whether via narratives, artwork, or firsthand accounts, Route 66 continues to be a vital and essential component of American cultural legacy.

Stories of People Who Shaped Route 66

Numerous people, among many others, had a significant influence in turning Route 66 into a well-known representation of opportunity, freedom, and adventure in the United States. Their efforts contributed to the establishment and maintenance of this historic roadway's cultural value, establishing a lasting legacy that draws travelers and enthusiasts from all over the world. Here are some stories of people who left their mark on this historic road:

Cyrus Avery - The Visionary Trailblazer

Meet Cyrus Avery, fondly known as the "Father of Route 66." A savvy businessman and politician, Avery's story unfolds within the corridors of the federal government's Joint Board on Interstate Highways. Picture him advocating passionately for a road that would connect the bustling city of Chicago to the sun-kissed shores of Los Angeles. Avery's vision and advocacy didn't just lay the foundations; they paved the way for the birth of this iconic roadway.

John T. Woodruff - The Heartland Advocate

In the heartland of Oklahoma, John T. Woodruff saw more than just stretches of land; he envisioned economic potential in the dusty trails that could become Route 66. Picture Woodruff as he tirelessly lobbied for the highway, ultimately giving birth to the U.S. 66 Highway Association. His dedication was not just about bricks and mortar; it was about fostering the promise that this road held for commerce and connectivity.

Angel Delgadillo - The Guardian Angel of the Iconic Route 66

Seligman, Arizona, found its guardian angel in the form of Angel Delgadillo. A humble barber, his family settled in the area when Route 66 was still in its infancy. Fast forward to the 1980s when the highway faced decommissioning; Delgadillo emerged as a champion for its preservation. Picture him rallying communities, establishing associations, and breathing new life into the historic road, ensuring that Route 66 remained not just a memory but a living legacy.

Bobby Troup - The Melodic Voyager

Enter the world of music with Bobby Troup, the man behind the classic anthem "Route 66." As a musician and songwriter, Troup's storytelling unfolded not in prose but in melodies. Imagine the resonance of his catchy tune echoing through the open roads, becoming an anthem for every traveler who ever set foot on the highway.

Jack D. Rittenhouse - The Highway Chronicler

In 1946, Jack D. Rittenhouse penned "A Guide Book to Highway 66," an essential companion for travelers navigating the twists and turns of Route 66.

Picture Rittenhouse as a guide, not just mapping out towns and attractions but weaving a narrative that made the highway come alive, promoting tourism and commerce with every word.

Landscapes and Geographical Features of Route 66 by Region

Route 66 takes you on an enthralling 2,448-mile (3,940-kilometer) journey across eight states in the United States. It starts in the dynamic city of Chicago, Illinois, and ends in the scenic Santa Monica, California. This famous route is a representation of the classic American road trip experience, winding through a rich tapestry of landscapes, natural wonders, and cultural sites in addition to connecting two far-off points.

Starting in the Midwest, in the states of Illinois and Missouri, the eastern stretch of Route 66 unfolds across the flat to gently rolling terrain of the region. Here, travelers are greeted by vast farmlands, charming small towns, and a plethora of historic sites. The landscape is adorned with agricultural fields, dense forests, and meandering rivers, creating a picturesque tableau that captures the essence of the heartland.

As the journey progresses westward through the Great Plains, encompassing Kansas, Oklahoma, and Texas, the topography becomes more varied and captivating. The route traverses wide-open prairies, rolling hills, and rugged landscapes, offering a distinct contrast to the Midwest. Notable geological features, including parts of the Ozark Plateau in Oklahoma and the Texas Panhandle, add a unique flavor to the scenery, providing travelers with breathtaking vistas and an immersive experience of America's vast and diverse landscapes.

Entering the Southwest, through the states of New Mexico and Arizona, Route 66 delves into the enchanting realm of desert landscapes and mesas, embodying the iconic imagery of the American West. The journey unfolds amidst vast expanses of arid terrain, featuring the high desert of New Mexico and the awe-inspiring landscapes of northern Arizona. This region boasts distinctive red rock formations, picturesque canyons, and historic trading posts that add to the allure of the journey.

The final leg of Route 66 in Southern California traverses the diverse landscapes of the West Coast. From the arid Mojave Desert to the coastal plains, travelers encounter a harmonious blend of desert scenery, majestic mountain ranges, and the captivating allure of the Pacific Ocean. The route concludes in Santa Monica, where the iconic Santa Monica Pier and the scenic coastline provide a fitting end to this epic cross-country adventure.

Key geographic features along the route include intersecting major rivers such as the Mississippi River in Illinois and Missouri, and the Rio Grande in New Mexico. Route 66 also passes near or through various mountain ranges, including the Ozarks in Missouri and Oklahoma, the Sangre de Cristo Mountains in New Mexico, and the San Gabriel Mountains in California. Notable national parks and monuments, such as Petrified Forest National Park in Arizona and Joshua Tree National Park in California, enhance the scenic beauty of the journey. Moreover, the route is adorned with historic landmarks, roadside attractions, and nostalgic remnants of America's automobile culture, contributing to the unique geography and cultural heritage of Route 66.

Languages Spoken in Regions and Communities Along the Route

As it winds through states like Illinois, Missouri, Kansas, Oklahoma, Texas, New Mexico, Arizona, and California, Route 66 is a well-known route that crosses a variety of American landscapes. This historic route connects rich cultural mosaics of communities whose language tapestry is reflected in its design.

Chicago, Illinois is a highly urbanized metropolis where English is the most widely spoken language. However, due to the city's rich immigration past, Spanish, Polish, and other Asian dialects are also spoken there, resulting in a diverse linguistic landscape. English is still widely used as one travels southwest into Missouri and Kansas. Still, remnants of the 19th-century European settlers can be found in communities with strong immigrant links, where pockets of German and French people still reside.

Native American languages like Cherokee coexist with English in tribal areas in Oklahoma, a state with a sizable Native American population. Although Spanish is widely spoken in Texas, a state that blends many cultures, English is the primary language, particularly in areas close to the Mexican border. Some communities have a strong European immigrant background, and German and Czech lend a historical touch.

Due in large part to the state's Hispanic population, Spanish becomes more often used as Route 66 enters New Mexico. Not to mention, tribal people still speak Native American languages like Navajo and Keres. English, Spanish, and Native American languages such as Hopi and Apache are blended together to create a linguistic landscape that embodies Arizona's rich cultural legacy. Spanish, Asian languages, and other languages are harmoniously blended with English, the state's predominant language, thanks to the state's immigrant past.

With Spanish, Native American, and European languages adding depth, English acts as the unifying language across these varied communities, creating an incredibly rich and singular cultural experience as one travels down the historic Route 66. This highway offers a sophisticated awareness of the places it connects, turning travel along it into a language voyage.

Useful Slangs and Phrases for First-time Travelers On Route 66

- "Get your kicks on Route 66" - Famous highway slogan.
- "Kitschy roadside attractions" - Quirky sights along the route.
- "Main Street of America" - Another nickname for Route 66.
- "Blue Plate Special" - Classic diner meal.
- "Two-lane blacktop" - Describes the road design.
- "Roadside Americana" - Unique elements along the highway.
- "Neon signs and vintage motels" - Retro business aesthetics.
- "Cruising the strip" - Leisurely driving through towns.
- "Bumper-to-bumper traffic" - Slow-moving traffic.

- "Gas up" - Fill up your gas tank.
- "Hit the brakes" - Slow down or stop.
- "Pit stop" - Quick break for gas or rest.
- "Punch it" - Accelerate quickly.
- "Backseat driver" - Someone giving unwanted advice while driving.
- "Rolling Thunder" - Group of motorcycles riding together.
- "Take a breather" - Take a break and relax.
- "Miles of smiles" - Joy while traveling Route 66.
- "Wind in your hair" - Feeling of freedom with windows down.
- "Rumble strips" - Noisy road patches indicating a hazard.
- "Keep on truckin'" - Keep moving forward.
- "Scenic overlook" - A place with a beautiful view.
- "Hitting the open highway" - Starting a long drive.

- "Motel hop" - Staying at different motels each night.
- "Buckle up for safety" - Remember to wear your seatbelt.
- "On the road again" - Ready to travel after a break.
- "Back in the saddle" - Ready to drive again after a break.
- "Rev up your engine" - Prepare to accelerate.
- "Out for a Sunday drive" - Leisurely drive without a destination.
- "Pit crew" - People helping during a road trip.
- "Hitchhiker's welcome" - Sign of hospitality.
- "Old-timer's tales" - Stories from residents and business owners.
- "Gravel cruncher" - Someone enjoying unpaved roads.

37

Chapter 2: Preparing for the Route 66 Adventure

When to Cruise Route 66

There are a number of things to take into account while deciding whether to travel along Route 66. Travelers often choose to visit during the spring, which runs from March to May, because of the pleasant weather, blooming wildflowers, and verdant surroundings. This time of year, when nature is at its most beautiful, is perfect for exploration and outdoor activities.

Even though the summer months of June through August are hot, they are the busiest travel times and draw tourists. To guarantee the greatest selection, travelers should book their lodging well in advance and be ready for packed attractions. Summer is a bright time to visit the famous roadway and all of its attractions since, in spite of the heat, it offers a bustling atmosphere.

Autumn, from September to November, offers a unique but no less captivating experience. The temperature drops, and the vivid fall foliage changes the surrounding vistas. For those looking for a more sedate and reflective road trip, this season is a great option because it offers a more laid-back ambiance than the hectic summer months.

Due to snow and icy conditions, winter, which lasts from December to February, can be difficult, especially in northern and hilly regions. For visitors hoping to see Route 66 in all its splendor, this season may provide fewer hours or perhaps be closed for some attractions. On the other hand, winter can be an exciting and less busy time to explore the ancient roadway for individuals who don't mind the weather.

When to travel may also be influenced by special occasions and celebrations of Route 66's history and culture. These activities can enhance your travel experience by giving you the ability to interact with locals and fully experience the distinct atmosphere of the path.

Choosing the Right Vehicle

One of the most important decisions in planning a successful and pleasurable trip down Route 66 is choosing the right vehicle. It is important to carefully evaluate a number of aspects while selecting the best kind of transportation for this famous road trip because Route 66 passes through a variety of terrains and road conditions.

The vehicle's dependability is the most important factor to take into account, because the route passes through a variety of environments, from crowded urban areas to isolated desert regions. For long trips and a range of road conditions, the selected car needs to show that it has a solid performance history and is durable enough to withstand the voyage without any problems.

Large and comfortable seats are important factors in improving the overall experience of traveling, in addition to dependability. Long stretches of time spent in the car are possible for visitors to Route 66, which winds across eight states and offers a plethora of attractions. Therefore, it becomes crucial to choose a roomy and comfortable car with lots of legroom, storage, and contemporary features.

Travel plans and personal tastes will determine whether to choose a camper van, SUV, or automobile. An SUV offers better off-road capabilities and more storage room for outdoor gear, but a car may be preferable due to its superior fuel efficiency and maneuverability in cities. By integrating lodging and transportation, on the other hand, a camper van offers a more adaptable and engaging travel experience.

The appeal of a vintage or classic car may be strong for individuals who are enthralled with Route 66's historical significance. But to withstand the hardships of the long trip, it is essential to make sure that these cars are properly maintained and outfitted.

Considering that the route passes through isolated locations with few gas stations, fuel efficiency becomes a realistic factor to keep expenses as low as possible. Purchasing a car with good gas mileage reduces gasoline costs and provides comfort while traveling long distances between fill-ups.

Airbags, anti-lock brakes, and stability control are among the safety measures that should receive the utmost consideration. In order to ensure a safe and secure travel along Route 66, vehicles with contemporary safety technologies must be given priority.

Budgeting and Costs

Setting off on an adventure along the renowned Route 66 is thrilling and demands careful budgetary planning to guarantee a smooth and pleasurable road trip, in addition to offering breathtaking scenery and a wealth of cultural diversity. Roadside attractions and charming motels can be found along this ancient route that winds across eight states to get to Santa Monica. So that you may maximize your Route 66 adventure, let's dive into some thorough financial concerns.

1. Accommodation:

Route 66 offers a diverse range of accommodation options, from charming motels to bed and breakfasts. Prices can vary, but budget-friendly options typically start around $50 to $100 per night. Consider booking in advance to secure the best rates, and explore unique lodging experiences that capture the spirit of Route 66.

2. Transportation:

Your primary mode of transportation will likely be a rental car for the ultimate Route 66 experience. Factor in rental costs, fuel expenses, and potential maintenance fees. To save on fuel, consider driving a fuel-efficient vehicle and plan your route with attention to gas station locations. Also, be aware of speed limits to avoid unnecessary fines. Rental car costs can range from $30 to $100 per day, depending on the type of vehicle.

3. Food and Dining:

Dining along Route 66 can range from classic diners to unique local eateries. Budget for meals at around $10 to $20 per person at more affordable establishments, while mid-range options may cost between $20 and $40. Save money by exploring local markets, trying regional specialties, and picnicking at scenic spots. Packing snacks for the road can also help control costs.

4. Attractions and Entertainment:

Route 66 is filled with quirky roadside attractions, historic landmarks, and museums. While some may have entry fees, many are free or request a voluntary donation. Plan your itinerary to include a mix of both paid and free attractions to balance your entertainment budget. Don't forget to budget for souvenirs to commemorate your journey.

5. Sightseeing Tours:

Route 66 is a self-guided adventure, but you might encounter guided tours or unique experiences along the way. Research and budget for any guided tours that align with your interests. However, keep in mind that much of the charm of Route 66 lies in discovering its hidden gems on your own.

6. Miscellaneous Expenses:

Account for miscellaneous expenses such as road tolls, parking fees, and unexpected vehicle-related costs. Setting aside a small contingency fund can help cover unforeseen circumstances and ensure a smoother journey.

7. Budgeting Apps and Tools:

Use budgeting apps or tools to track your daily expenses on the road. This will help you stay on budget and make adjustments as needed. Inputting your spending regularly will give you a clear picture of your financial status throughout the trip.

8. Emergency Fund:

Always have a small emergency fund for unexpected situations, whether it's a flat tire or a sudden detour. This fund can provide peace of mind and help you navigate unexpected challenges without disrupting your travel plans. Consider setting aside $100 to $200 for emergency expenses.

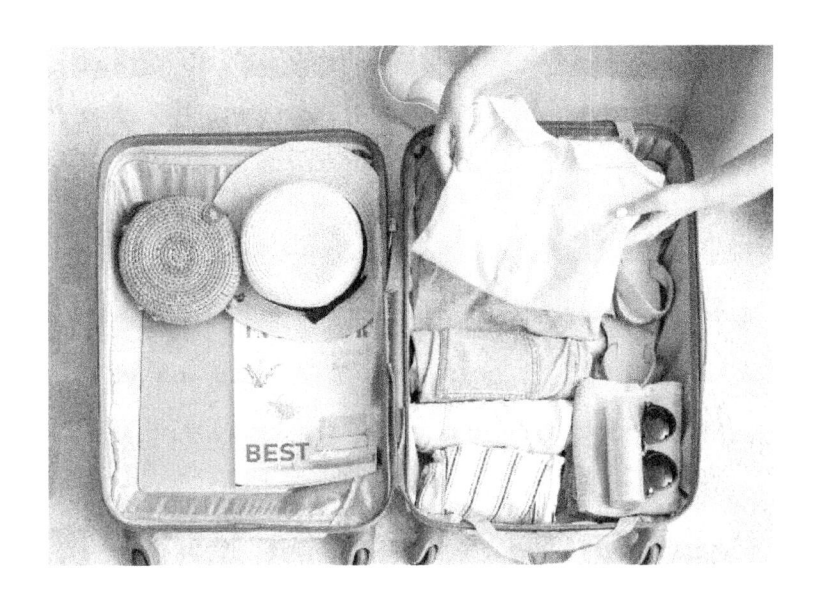

What to Pack

When planning a vacation along Route 66, travelers should take into account the variety of landscapes, climates, and activities that can be found along this historic route. A comfortable and joyful journey is contingent upon being well-prepared with the necessary gear and requirements, whether one is traveling through urban cityscapes or lonely desert expanses. Here is a thorough packing list for a road trip along Route 66:

1. Clothing:

Comfortable Walking Shoes: Given the potential for exploring attractions, historical sites, and natural landmarks, sturdy and comfortable walking shoes are a must.

Lightweight Clothing: Pack a mix of lightweight, breathable clothing suitable for warm temperatures, including t-shirts, shorts, and sundresses.

Layered Clothing: Route 66 spans multiple states with varying climates, so packing layers such as long-sleeve shirts, sweaters, and jackets is essential for cooler evenings or unexpected weather changes.

Rain Gear: A lightweight, packable rain jacket or poncho can come in handy, especially during the rainy season or in regions prone to sudden showers.

2. Travel Accessories:

Sun Protection: Bring sunscreen, sunglasses, and a wide-brimmed hat to shield against the sun's rays, particularly in the open landscapes of the Southwest.

Insect Repellent: Some areas along Route 66 may have mosquitoes or other biting insects, so packing insect repellent is advisable.

Travel-sized First Aid Kit: Include basic medical supplies such as adhesive bandages, antiseptic wipes, pain relievers, and any necessary prescription medications.

Travel Documents: Pack important documents such as driver's license, passport (if traveling internationally), insurance information, and any reservation confirmations.

3. Electronics and Gadgets:

Camera or Smartphone: Capture the scenic landscapes and iconic landmarks along Route 66 with a camera or smartphone equipped with a quality camera.

Portable Charger: Ensure that electronic devices stay charged by packing a portable charger or power bank for on-the-go recharging.

GPS or Navigation App: While many travelers use smartphones for navigation, it's a good idea to have a backup GPS device or printed maps in case of limited cellular coverage in remote areas.

4. Outdoor Gear:

Daypack or Backpack: A lightweight daypack is useful for carrying water bottles, snacks, maps, and other essentials during outdoor excursions or hikes.

Water Bottle: Stay hydrated by bringing a reusable water bottle to refill at various stops along the route.

Hiking Gear: If planning to explore national parks or hiking trails, consider packing hiking boots, trekking poles, and appropriate outdoor gear.

5. Road Trip Essentials:

Car Emergency Kit: Pack essentials such as jumper cables, tire pressure gauge, flashlight with extra batteries, and a basic toolkit for minor vehicle repairs.

Travel Snacks: Stock up on non-perishable snacks like trail mix, granola bars, and fruit to keep energy levels up during long drives.

Entertainment: Bring along books, audiobooks, music playlists, or travel games to keep entertained during road trips between destinations.

6. Miscellaneous Items:

Reusable Shopping Bags: Useful for carrying groceries or souvenirs obtained along the route.

Travel Towel: A compact, quick-drying travel towel can be handy for impromptu picnics or visits to beaches or swimming holes.

Ziplock Bags: These versatile bags can be used for storing snacks, organizing small items, or protecting electronics from dust and moisture.

By packing thoughtfully with these essentials in mind, travelers can ensure they are well-prepared for the diverse experiences and environments encountered while traveling along Route 66. It's also advisable to check the specific weather forecasts and local conditions for the planned travel dates to make any necessary adjustments to the packing list.

Fuel and Service Costs

As travelers venture along the historic expanse of Route 66, understanding the dynamics of fluctuating fuel prices and the varied costs associated with automotive services becomes paramount for a journey marked by both smooth transitions and financial prudence. Throughout the diverse array of fuel and service stations peppering the route, a trend of competitive pricing generally prevails, offering a reassuring prospect for those traversing this iconic road.

Fuel prices exhibit a range for regular unleaded gasoline between $2.50 and $3.50 per gallon. This spectrum is shaped by an intricate interplay of regional fuel taxes, market demand fluctuations, and the proximity to major metropolitan areas. For those seeking alternatives, mid-grade and premium gasoline options are readily available, though at a slightly escalated cost, with an additional expenditure of approximately $0.20 to $0.60 per gallon compared to the regular unleaded counterpart.

Diesel fuel, often a necessity for certain vehicles, inhabits a pricing realm between $2.80 and $3.80 per gallon. The variability in this range is influenced by local supply and demand dynamics, further nuanced by seasonal factors impacting diesel consumption.

Turning our attention to the realm of automotive services, costs at Route 66 service stations and repair shops are subject to an amalgamation of factors. In the current landscape, approximate costs for common automotive services unfold as follows:

- Standard oil changes are typically priced between $30 and $50, while synthetic oil changes may cost $50 to $70 due to the higher cost of synthetic oil.
- Tire rotation services are generally priced in the range of $20 to $40, depending on the shop's labor rates and any additional services included in the package.
- Basic repairs, such as brake pad replacement, battery replacement, or belt replacement, may cost between $100 and $300. Costs depend

on the specific repair needed and the parts and labor involved.
- Other services, such as car washes, tire repairs, and diagnostic checks, can vary widely based on the specific service provider and the level of service offered.

Emphasizing that these pricing ranges are estimates is important because they could change depending on specific service providers, region, and the always fluctuating market conditions. In order to ensure accurate cost estimates that are in line with their particular travel needs, travelers are strongly recommended to inquire about current pricing at various gas and service stations along Route 66. Moreover, utilizing the benefits of loyalty programs, discounts, and exclusive offers from gas stations and service providers might be a smart way to save costs on this legendary trip.

Environmental Considerations

As the popularity of Route 66 grows, so does the concern about its environmental impact, echoing the delicate balance between preservation and the effects of increased tourism and vehicular traffic. Through the implementation of sustainable practices, active conservation efforts, and heightened awareness of environmental considerations, this historic highway can continue to be a cherished destination for future generations, preserving its natural beauty and ecological integrity for years to come. Here, we delve into several environmental considerations associated with this route.

1. Air Quality:

The surge in vehicular traffic along Route 66 contributes significantly to air pollution, especially in urban areas and popular tourist destinations. The emissions from cars, trucks, and motorcycles pose threats to air quality, potentially leading to adverse health effects and environmental degradation. Initiatives promoting carpooling, the adoption of electric vehicles, and the use of public transportation can play a pivotal role in mitigating the impact on air quality.

2. Wildlife Habitat:

The diverse landscapes encompassed by Route 66, ranging from deserts and grasslands to forests, serve as vital habitats for various plant and animal species. However, heightened human activity along the route poses a risk to these ecosystems, causing habitat disruption, fragmentation, and a loss of biodiversity. Conservation measures, such as wildlife corridors and protected areas, are essential to offsetting the impact on local ecosystems.

3. Waste Management:

The increase in tourism brings with it a surge in waste generated by roadside businesses, restaurants, and lodging facilities along Route 66. Proper waste management practices, including comprehensive recycling programs and dedicated litter cleanup initiatives, are imperative to maintain the scenic beauty and ecological integrity of the route.

4. Water Conservation:

Water scarcity is a pressing issue in many regions along Route 66, particularly in the arid Southwest. The influx of tourists can strain local water resources, risking overuse and potential depletion of aquifers and rivers. Implementing sustainable water management practices, such as water conservation measures and responsible irrigation techniques, is vital for preserving the delicate balance of water ecosystems.

5. Historic Preservation:

Numerous historic sites and landmarks dot the landscape along Route 66, each carrying its own set of environmental considerations. Striking a balance between the need to protect these cultural treasures and adopting sustainable practices that minimize the impact on surrounding ecosystems is crucial for long-term preservation efforts.

6. Renewable Energy:

Encouraging the use of renewable energy sources, such as solar and wind power, along Route 66 can substantially reduce reliance on fossil fuels and cut down greenhouse gas emissions. The integration of solar panels and wind turbines at rest stops and visitor centers not only showcases sustainable energy solutions but also actively contributes to decreasing the environmental footprint of the route.

Road Conditions and Weather Challenges

Each of Route 66's regions and scenery presents a different set of weather-related road conditions. Travelers experience a variety of environments as they go along this iconic highway, from the arid deserts of the Southwest to the urban streets of Chicago. A safe and enjoyable trip along Route 66 requires an understanding of the weather and road conditions.

Road Conditions:

The road conditions along Route 66 vary widely, as the highway traverses through multiple states with diverse terrains. In some areas, the highway is well-maintained and modernized, providing a smooth and comfortable driving experience. However, in other segments, particularly those known as "The Historic Route 66," travelers may encounter historic two-lane roads with more rustic conditions, including uneven surfaces, occasional potholes, and narrower lanes.

Furthermore, some sections of Route 66 have been bypassed by interstate highways, resulting in partial or complete abandonment. While efforts have been made to preserve and maintain the historic route, these abandoned segments may pose challenges such as deteriorated road surfaces and limited services.

In addition to the varying road conditions, travelers should be prepared for road construction and maintenance activities, which can impact traffic flow and travel times. It is advisable for travelers to stay informed about road closures, detours, and construction updates to plan their journey effectively.

Weather Challenges:

Weather along Route 66 can present diverse challenges due to the range of climates and landscapes traversed by the highway. From the temperate climate of the Midwest to the arid deserts of the Southwest, travelers should be prepared for a wide spectrum of weather conditions.

During the summer months, travelers in the southwestern states, such as Arizona and California, may encounter extremely high temperatures, often exceeding 100°F (38°C). This intense heat can pose challenges for vehicle cooling systems and require extra precautions to avoid overheating.

Conversely, in the northern regions, particularly Illinois and Missouri, travelers may encounter inclement weather such as heavy rains and thunderstorms, which can impact visibility and road conditions. Flooding is a particular concern in low-lying areas and near rivers during periods of heavy rainfall.

In the winter months, parts of Route 66, especially in the higher elevations of Arizona and California, may experience snow and ice, leading to slippery road conditions and reduced visibility. Travelers should be prepared for the possibility of winter weather and should carry appropriate supplies, such as tire chains and emergency kits, if journeying during the colder season.

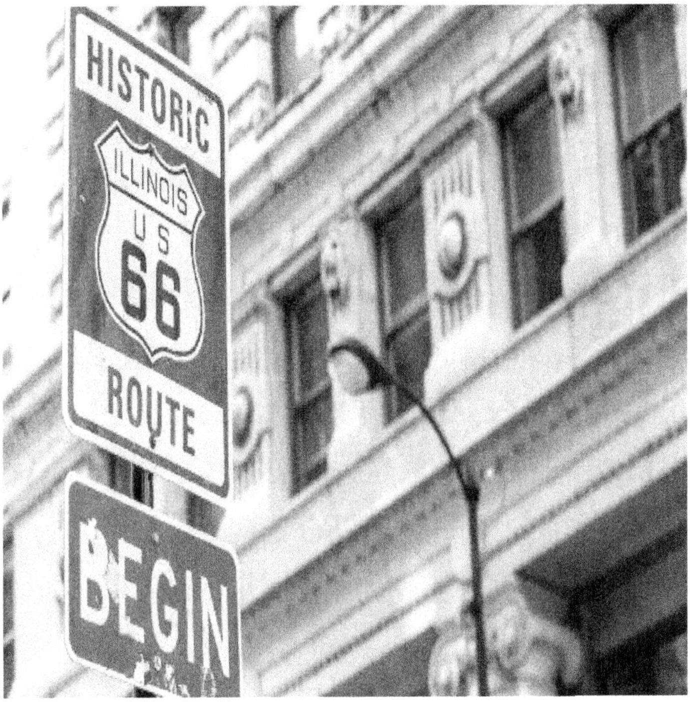
HISTORIC
ILLINOIS
U S
66
ROUTE
BEGIN

Chapter 3: Navigating Route 66

Starting Points

Although Route 66 was formally discontinued as a U.S. highway in 1985, its legacy endures, attracting tourists and enthusiasts interested in exploring its historic route and diverse landscapes. Its starting points, traditionally associated with Chicago, Illinois, in the east, and Santa Monica, California, in the west, which have undergone debate and variation due to the evolving alignment of the highway. Travelers today can experience a blend of historic sites, roadside attractions, and the evolving American landscape that has made Route 66 a lasting symbol of adventure and exploration.

Chicago, Illinois (Eastern Starting Point)

In downtown Chicago, near Lake Michigan, the intersection of Adams Street and Michigan Avenue stands as the widely accepted eastern terminus of Route 66. This locale carries profound historical weight, serving as the starting point for numerous travelers during the heyday of Route 66. The journey officially begins with the unmistakable "Begin Route 66" sign, an iconic marker that sets the stage for the adventure ahead. Noteworthy landmarks in Chicago linked to Route 66 include the Art Institute of Chicago, Grant Park, and Buckingham Fountain.

Santa Monica, California (Western Terminus)

On the western horizon, the Santa Monica Pier in California stands as the revered conclusion of Route

66. This coastal landmark, basking in an iconic atmosphere, signifies the end of the cross-country odyssey for those traveling from east to west. Santa Monica, renowned for its scenic beach and historic pier, encapsulates the fulfillment of the extensive road trip, embodying the evolution of American leisure and recreation culture. The Santa Monica Pier Aquarium and the historic Looff Hippodrome Carousel add unique cultural dimensions to the coastal endpoint, enhancing the overall experience for explorers.

Ending Points

The ending points of Route 66, located on opposite coasts of the United States, hold distinct significance in the collective memory of travelers and enthusiasts who have traversed this iconic highway.

Santa Monica, California (Eastern Starting Point)

In the opposite direction, the Santa Monica Pier in California serves as the initial point of Route 66 for those heading eastward. Nestled against the picturesque beach with its historic charm, this iconic pier symbolizes the genesis of the cross-country journey and reflects the diverse cultural influences that contribute to the vibrant tapestry of Route 66. The California Incline, a historic roadway connecting the Pacific Coast Highway to Ocean Avenue in Santa Monica, plays a pivotal role, serving as a gateway to the coastal starting point, setting the stage for the adventure ahead.

Chicago, Illinois (Western Terminus)

Starting from Chicago and heading west, Route 66 passes through Illinois, Missouri, Kansas, Oklahoma, Texas, New Mexico, and Arizona before concluding its iconic journey at the Santa Monica Pier in California. Along each mile, you experience classic American scenes with charming small towns and nostalgic attractions. The special appeal of Route 66 comes from the memories created along the way, celebrating freedom and exploration. Even though modern highways are more practical, Route 66 still represents the American dream and the adventurous spirit of the open road. Ending at the Pacific Ocean, the Santa Monica Pier, with its "End of the Trail" sign, connects with the emotions of countless explorers. As the sun sets, Route 66 transforms from a physical journey into a timeless adventure.

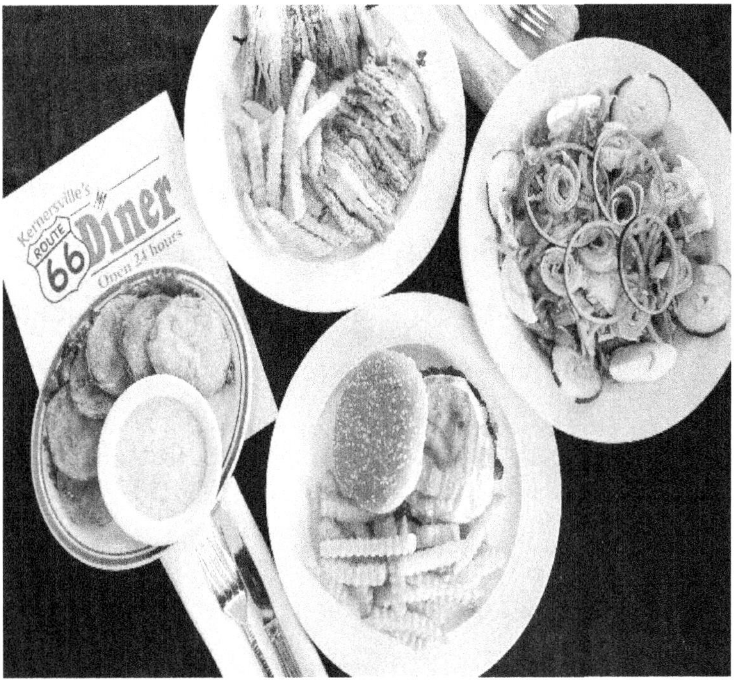
Kernersville's
ROUTE
66
Diner
Open 24 hours

Chapter 4: Regional Food and Drink Options Along Route 66

Traveling along the famous Route 66 is more than simply seeing the country's wide landscapes; it's also a chance to explore the cuisine, which reflects the rich cultural diversity of the country. The rich history and distinctive culinary cultures of Chicago, Illinois, provide the backdrop for an amazing journey as you travel the historic route.

The hearty flavors of the Midwest are first introduced to you in Chicago, home of the famous hot dogs and deep-dish pizza. After that, the voyage reveals the unique sounds of St. Louis's cuisine, allowing you to relish BBQ flavors and take in the city's culinary pulse. Your gastronomic excursion is enhanced by each location along the way, weaving together a tapestry of flavors that pays homage to the richness of American history.

Get ready for a visual and culinary feast as you explore Texas' enormous landscapes. The state's well-known barbecue customs, which offer a distinctive fusion of flavors that convey the tale of the Lone Star State, go well with the vast vistas. Oklahoma opens your eyes to a variety of regional specialties, from distinctive local delicacies to hearty comfort dishes.

The Southwestern charm of Arizona and New Mexico adds a spark of heat to your gastronomic exploration. With dishes like green chiles and southwestern-style cooking, these states provide a glimpse of the colorful and energetic culture of the area. As you discover the distinctive flavors that characterize the Southwest, your taste buds will dance to the beat of the desert.

Your culinary adventure comes to an end in Santa Monica, California, a laid-back beach resort that offers the ideal setting for thinking back on the variety of flavors you have encountered. Route 66 has knitted together a story that transcends the landscape, capturing the spirit of the people and their stories through the lens of cuisine, from iconic diners to hidden roadside treasures.

<u>Chicago, Illinois</u>:

Food:

- Deep-dish pizza - Thick crust, layers of cheese, and hearty tomato sauce.
- Chicago-style hot dogs - Mustard, onions, sweet pickle relish, dill pickle spear, tomatoes, sport peppers, and celery salt on a poppy seed bun.

Drinks:

- Thriving craft beer scene - Explore local breweries with a variety of craft brews.

Illinois:

Food:

- Horseshoe sandwich - Springfield specialty with ham, turkey, or hamburger patties.
- Italian beef sandwich - Thinly sliced roast beef on an Italian roll with sweet peppers or spicy giardiniera.

Drinks:

- Historic breweries - Dive into the rich beer culture of the state.

Missouri:

Food:

- St. Louis-style barbecue ribs - Slow-cooked pork with tangy barbecue sauce.
- Local soul food - Fried catfish and crispy fried chicken.

Drinks:

- Historic breweries and family-owned diners - Discover local libations.

Oklahoma:

Food:

- Chicken-fried steak - Breaded and fried beef cutlet with creamy gravy.
- Hearty chili and pecan pie - Southern comfort food.

Drinks:

- Artisanal spirits - Immerse yourself in the local spirit scene.

Texas:

Food:

- Tex-Mex delights - Fajitas, enchiladas, tacos, and legendary barbecue with slow-smoked brisket and ribs.

Drinks:

- Vast Texan wine country - Explore local wines to complement your culinary journey.

New Mexico:

Food:

- Southwestern cuisine - Green and red chile peppers in enchiladas, carne adovada (marinated pork slow-cooked in red chile sauce).

Drinks:

- Burgeoning wine scene - Sip on regional wines.

Arizona:

Food:

- Sonoran-style Mexican cuisine - Bacon-wrapped Sonoran hot dogs, tamales, and carne asada tacos.

Drinks:

- Unique flavors of Arizona's wine country - Explore local wines.

California (Santa Monica):
Food:
- Iconic West Coast fare - Fresh seafood and In-N-Out Burger.

Drinks:
- Coastal culinary scene - Indulge in a variety of seafood dishes.

Libations Along the Route:
- Regional craft beers, historic breweries, and unique spirits in various states.
- Local wines in each state, showcasing the unique flavors of the region.

83

Chapter 5: Accommodation Options

You will have the chance to select from a broad range of lodging options along Route 66, each of which will suit your own interests and likes. These choices add to the overall thrill of your trip, each as varied as the scenery and points of interest that the historic route passes through. Here's a thorough rundown of places to stay along the famous route:

1. Historic Motels and Motor Courts:

Route 66 is renowned for its classic motels and motor courts that evoke the nostalgia of a bygone era. Many of these establishments have been lovingly restored to their mid-20th-century charm, offering travelers a unique opportunity to experience retro Americana. These accommodations often feature neon signs, vintage décor, and a welcoming, community-oriented atmosphere. Some well-known examples include the Blue Swallow Motel in

Tucumcari, New Mexico, and the Wigwam Motel in Holbrook, Arizona, where guests can stay in teepee-shaped rooms.

2. Bed and Breakfasts:

Along the route, you'll find charming bed and breakfast establishments that provide a more intimate and personalized lodging experience. These accommodations are often housed in historic buildings and offer cozy rooms, home-cooked breakfasts, and attentive hospitality. Bed and breakfasts along Route 66 may be located in quaint small towns or rural settings, providing a peaceful retreat for travelers looking to unwind and enjoy the local ambiance.

3. Modern Hotels and Resorts:

For those seeking contemporary amenities and comfort, there are numerous modern hotels and resorts situated along Route 66. These accommodations range from budget-friendly chain hotels to upscale resorts with luxurious facilities. Travelers can expect features such as swimming pools, fitness centers, on-site dining options, and spacious rooms equipped with modern conveniences. Many of these properties cater to both leisure and business travelers, offering a full range of services and amenities.

4. Campgrounds and RV Parks:

Camping enthusiasts and road trippers with recreational vehicles can take advantage of the various campgrounds and RV parks located near Route 66. These options provide an opportunity to immerse oneself in the natural beauty of the surrounding landscapes while enjoying outdoor activities. Campgrounds may offer tent sites, RV hookups, picnic areas, and facilities such as restrooms and showers. Some locations also organize group activities and events for guests.

5. Unique Accommodations:

Along Route 66, travelers can find an array of unique lodging options that add an extra element of adventure to their journey. This includes themed motels, quirky roadside attractions with overnight accommodations, and even lodging in historic train cars or cabooses. Unconventional accommodations provide an opportunity for memorable experiences and are often located near iconic landmarks or points of interest along the route.

6. Booking Considerations:

When planning your stay along Route 66, it's advisable to book accommodations in advance, especially during peak travel seasons or at popular destinations. Many historic motels and unique lodgings have limited availability due to their distinct appeal. Additionally, consider factors such as pet-friendly policies, accessibility for individuals with disabilities, and proximity to attractions or dining options when selecting your lodging.

89

Chapter 6: Outdoor and Recreational Activities

Even the most seasoned travelers might become restless when stuck in a car for a long distance. Thus, scheduling some time to spend outside and away from the car is always a smart idea. For those who enjoy the outdoors and history, as well as those who are looking for adventure and relaxation, there are a plethora of outdoor and recreational activities along Route 66 that you may include in your vacation schedule. These excursions provide visitors with a wide variety of experiences amid the famed highway's natural beauty and cultural attractions. Here are some of the things to do along the Mother Road, ranging from hiking and camping to breathtaking drives and historic exploration:

1. Hiking and Nature Trails:

The enchanting landscapes traversed by Route 66 create an ideal setting for hiking and nature exploration. As travelers wind through the Grand Canyon, Petrified Forest National Park, and Joshua Tree National Park, they are presented with a myriad of scenic trails, each weaving a unique tale of the natural beauty inherent in the American Southwest.

2. Camping and RV Adventures:

Route 66 unveils numerous camping and RV sites, providing outdoor enthusiasts with an opportunity to immerse themselves in the rugged beauty of the countryside. Whether setting up camp along the banks of the Colorado River in Arizona or basking under the starry skies of New Mexico, camping along Route 66 offers a serene departure into the hug of nature.

3. Scenic Drives:

The very essence of Route 66 lies in the open road, offering a picturesque journey through diverse landscapes, from the rolling hills of Illinois to the arid deserts of California. Travelers can indulge in leisurely drives, absorbing the ever-changing scenery and pausing at iconic landmarks like the eccentric Cadillac Ranch in Texas or the historic Santa Monica Pier in California.

4. Historic Landmarks and Museums:

Lineated with historic landmarks, museums, and roadside attractions, Route 66 serves as a living testament to the cultural heritage of America. The Route 66 Museum in Oklahoma, the Wigwam Motel in Arizona, and the Lincoln Home National Historic Site in Illinois beckon visitors to delve into the rich history and nostalgic charm that the Mother Road embodies.

5. Cycling and Motorcycle Tours:

For those seeking an exhilarating journey on two wheels, Route 66 opens its arms to cycling enthusiasts and motorcycle riders alike. Cyclists pedal through scenic byways and charming towns, while motorcyclists revel in the freedom of the open road, with options to join organized tours or chart their own course along this iconic route.

6. Wildlife Watching and Photography:

The diverse ecosystems flanking Route 66 create a haven for wildlife watching and photography enthusiasts. From spotting majestic bison herds in Oklahoma to capturing the vibrant beauty of wildflowers in New Mexico, nature enthusiasts can submerge themselves in the natural splendor of the landscapes that border this historic highway.

7. Water Activities:

Certain segments of Route 66 unfold opportunities for water-based activities such as kayaking, fishing, and boating. The Colorado River, snaking through Arizona and California, along with lakes and reservoirs in states like Oklahoma and New Mexico, beckon travelers to indulge in aquatic adventures surrounded by stunning natural vistas.

8. Stargazing and Night Sky Viewing:

Embraced by wide-open spaces and minimal light pollution in certain areas, Route 66 emerges as an ideal canvas for stargazing and observing the night sky. Travelers can leverage designated stargazing areas or simply pull over at scenic spots, allowing them to marvel at the celestial wonders that adorn the vast expanse above.

Chapter 7: Sightseeing

Side Trips from Route 66

There are a lot of side trips and sights along Route 66's 2,448-mile route that provide visitors the chance to learn about the varied landscapes, cultures, and histories of the United States. These extended side trips provide a rich tapestry of experiences, ranging from historical sites and cultural treasures to natural wonders and geological marvels. If you take the time to get off Route 66, you'll find that the experience truly begins off its asphalt. Here are a few interesting detours:

Taos Pueblo - New Mexico

A side trip to Taos Pueblo, a UNESCO World Heritage Site, is a journey back in time. This living Native American community, with its multi-story adobe dwellings, preserves centuries-old traditions. Explore the narrow alleys, attend traditional ceremonies, and immerse yourself in the rich cultural tapestry.

Hoover Dam - Nevada/Arizona Border

A deviation to the Hoover Dam, straddling the Nevada-Arizona border, showcases engineering prowess amid breathtaking surroundings. Take a guided tour to learn about its construction, marvel at its scale, and witness the serene beauty of the Colorado River.*

Acoma Pueblo - New Mexico

A detour to Acoma Pueblo, also known as "Sky City," provides a unique encounter with one of the oldest continuously inhabited communities in North America. Perched atop a mesa, the pueblo offers guided tours, showcasing traditional adobe architecture and a rich cultural heritage.

Grand Canyon National Park, Arizona

A detour from Route 66 leads to the awe-inspiring Grand Canyon, a geological marvel that defies description. The panoramic vistas, hiking trails along the rim, and exhilarating helicopter tours provide visitors with a profound connection to nature's grandeur.

Meteor Crater, Arizona

Nestled near Winslow, Arizona, Meteor Crater stands as a testament to the colossal impact of a meteorite nearly 50,000 years ago. Venture to the rim to witness the vastness of this crater and delve into the captivating history of this extraordinary geological formation.

Petrified Forest National Park, Arizona

Just a short distance from Route 66, Petrified Forest National Park unveils a prehistoric landscape adorned with ancient petrified wood and vibrant badlands. Exploring this natural wonder exposes visitors to historical sites, including petroglyphs and Puebloan ruins.

Carlsbad Caverns National Park, New Mexico

Venturing southward from Route 66 leads to Carlsbad Caverns, an underground marvel teeming with stunning caves and unique rock formations. Witnessing the breathtaking bat flight at sunset adds a surreal dimension to this subterranean wonderland.

Monuments and Memorials Along the Route

Rich memorials and monuments that serve as moving memories of America's past can be found all along Route 66. Numerous historical markers, monuments, and memorial buildings that are encountered by drivers on this well-known roadway add to the Mother Road's story. Travelers are encouraged to connect with history and recognize the significance of this fabled roadway by each one, which adds to a larger story. So let's have a look at a few of the noteworthy memorials and monuments along Route 66:

1. Cyrus Avery Centennial Plaza - Tulsa, Oklahoma:

Dedicated to Cyrus Avery, often referred to as the "Father of Route 66," this plaza in Tulsa celebrates Avery's pivotal role in the establishment of the Mother Road. Featuring sculptures and exhibits, it provides insights into the history and significance of Route 66.

2. Gateway Arch, St. Louis, Missouri:

The Gateway Arch, designed by architect Eero Saarinen, stands as an iconic symbol of westward expansion in the United States. Soaring to 630 feet, it is the tallest man-made monument in the country. The Arch, located on the banks of the Mississippi River, offers a unique tram ride to an observation deck, providing stunning views of St. Louis. The Museum of Westward Expansion beneath the Arch explores the history of America's westward expansion, making this monument a captivating blend of architectural brilliance and historical significance.

3. Veterans Memorial Park - Albuquerque, New Mexico:

An expansive park in Albuquerque dedicated to honoring the veterans of the United States. The memorial features monuments, sculptures, and plaques paying tribute to the men and women who served in the armed forces.

4. Wupatki National Monument - Arizona:

Located northeast of Flagstaff, Wupatki National Monument is an archaeological marvel that invites travelers to explore the remnants of ancient Puebloan dwellings. The centerpiece, Wupatki Pueblo, showcases intricate stone masonry and reveals the advanced architectural techniques of the ancestral Puebloan people who inhabited the region over 800 years ago. The monument encompasses several sites, including the Citadel Pueblo and the Box Canyon Pueblo, each offering a glimpse into the daily lives and cultural richness of the indigenous communities. Petroglyphs, ancient artifacts, and a visitor center further enhance the educational experience, making Wupatki National Monument a significant stop along Route 66 for those seeking a deeper understanding of the Southwest's pre-Columbian history.

5. Chain of Rocks Bridge - St. Louis, Missouri:

As an iconic symbol of Route 66, the Chain of Rocks Bridge is a monument to the early days of the highway and the challenges of crossing the mighty Mississippi River. The bridge, featuring a unique 22-degree turn, served as a crucial river crossing for travelers on Route 66. Today, it stands not only as a testament to engineering achievements but also as a reminder of the road's historical significance in connecting the eastern and western parts of the United States.

6. Standin' on a Corner Park - Winslow, Arizona:

Winslow, Arizona, gained worldwide recognition thanks to the Eagles' hit song "Take It Easy," which famously includes the line "standin' on a corner in Winslow, Arizona." In homage to this cultural connection, Standin' on a Corner Park was established. This charming park serves as a monument to the impact of Route 66 on popular culture. Visitors can stand on the corner, take in murals depicting the song's lyrics, and reflect on the enduring legacy of the Mother Road.

7. Route 66 "End of the Trail" - Santa Monica Pier, California:

As travelers reach the western terminus of Route 66, the "End of the Trail" sign at Santa Monica Pier serves as a monumental marker, symbolizing the completion of the cross-country journey. This landmark holds a special place in the hearts of those who have traversed the entire length of Route 66, marking the end of an iconic road trip and a celebration of the American spirit.

Museums and Galleries Along the Route

A fascinating trip through time, history, and Americana is provided by the numerous museums and galleries along the historic Route 66. These organizations preserve history and tell the numerous stories that have come to pass along the Mother Road. Through interactive exhibitions and vintage cars, they enhance the Mother Road experience and let visitors immerse themselves in the many stories that have shaped this famous route. In-depth examination of a few of the galleries and museums that enhance the Route 66 experience is what we will be doing here.

1. Route 66 Interpretive Center - Chandler, Oklahoma:

In Chandler, Oklahoma, the Route 66 Interpretive Center offers a deep dive into the culture and heritage of the Mother Road. This center houses exhibits that explore the evolution of Route 66, from its early days to its heyday as the Main Street of America. Interactive displays engage visitors in the sights and sounds of the iconic highway, providing a comprehensive understanding of its significance in American history.

2. National Route 66 and Transportation Museum - Elk City, Oklahoma:

Elk City's National Route 66 and Transportation Museum serves as a comprehensive showcase of the evolution of transportation along Route 66. Vintage cars, memorabilia, and exhibits depict the heyday of the Mother Road, offering visitors a glimpse into the changing modes of travel and the cultural impact of this historic highway. The museum's curated collection captures the spirit of the road's golden era.

3. California Route 66 Museum - Victorville, California:

As travelers approach the western end of Route 66, the California Route 66 Museum in Victorville becomes a focal point. This museum delves into the road's significance in California's history, featuring exhibits on the Dust Bowl migration, the rise of roadside culture, and the enduring allure of the Mother Road. The museum's collections provide a nuanced perspective on the cultural and social changes along this iconic route.

4. Barstow Route 66 "Mother Road" Museum - California:

Located in Barstow, California, the "Mother Road" Museum celebrates the cultural and historical impact of Route 66. Exhibits cover a broad range of topics, including early pioneers, Native American history, and the road's significance during the Great Depression. The museum serves as a vibrant cultural hub, preserving the diverse history of the Mother Road and offering insights into the lives of those who traveled it.

5. Illinois Route 66 Hall of Fame and Museum - Pontiac, Illinois:

In Pontiac, Illinois, the Illinois Route 66 Hall of Fame and Museum pays homage to individuals who made significant contributions to the development and preservation of Route 66. The museum features exhibits that highlight the stories of those who left an indelible mark on the highway, creating a captivating narrative of the road's evolution.

6. Oklahoma Route 66 Museum - Clinton, Oklahoma:

The Oklahoma Route 66 Museum in Clinton, Oklahoma, is an immersive experience that transports visitors back to the heyday of the Mother Road. With engaging exhibits, artifacts, and interactive displays, the museum unfolds the stories of the people and places along Route 66. It serves as a dynamic tribute to the road's cultural significance and the lives touched by its asphalt ribbon.

Roadside Americanas

Route 66 is also well-known for its colorful and eccentric roadside attractions, which have evolved into well-known icons of American culture.

These roadside Americanas give passengers a nostalgic and engaging experience while also adding character to the trip. Let's take a closer look at a few of the noteworthy side attractions along Route 66:

1. The Blue Whale - Catoosa, Oklahoma:

Nestled in Catoosa, Oklahoma, the Blue Whale is a whimsical and colossal roadside attraction that has become a beloved symbol of Route 66. Originally built as a surprise anniversary gift, this 80-foot-long blue whale invites travelers to explore its interior and bask in its unique charm. The site includes picnic areas, making it a perfect spot for a roadside break and a memorable photo opportunity.

2. Cadillac Ranch - Amarillo, Texas:

Amarillo, Texas, is home to the iconic Cadillac Ranch, an art installation featuring ten half-buried Cadillac cars, nose-down in the ground. Created in 1974 by the art collective Ant Farm, this installation has become a symbol of the free-spirited and creative nature of Route 66. Visitors are encouraged to bring spray paint and leave their mark on the cars, making it an ever-evolving and participatory roadside art piece.

3. Wigwam Village Motel - Holbrook, Arizona:

The Wigwam Village Motel in Holbrook, Arizona, is a classic example of roadside Americana. This unique motel features individual rooms housed within teepee-shaped structures, offering travelers a taste of vintage roadside lodging. Built in the 1930s, the Wigwam Village Motel is a nostalgic reminder of the quirky and distinctive accommodations that once dotted the landscape along Route 66.

4. Blue Swallow Motel - Tucumcari, New Mexico:

The Blue Swallow Motel in Tucumcari, New Mexico, is not just a place to rest; it's a living relic of the golden era of Route 66. Known for its neon-lit sign and meticulously preserved retro rooms, the Blue Swallow Motel harks back to the heyday of the Mother Road. Travelers can experience the charm of mid-century hospitality while reveling in the nostalgia of this roadside gem.

5. The Big Texan Steak Ranch - Amarillo, Texas:

Amarillo's Big Texan Steak Ranch is not just a restaurant; it's a legendary stop along Route 66. Home to the famous "72 oz. Steak Challenge," this establishment embraces the larger-than-life spirit of the American West. The iconic neon sign, cowboy-themed decor, and the promise of a free meal for those who can finish the colossal steak contribute to the allure of this roadside institution.

6. Route 66 Drive-In Theatre - Carthage, Missouri:

The Route 66 Drive-In Theatre in Carthage, Missouri, is a nostalgic tribute to the bygone era of outdoor cinema. Operating since 1949, it provides a unique cinematic experience under the stars, allowing travelers to relive the classic charm of drive-in theaters that were once synonymous with Route 66.

7. The Gemini Giant - Wilmington, Illinois:

The Gemini Giant in Wilmington, Illinois, is a towering fiberglass figure that stands as a guardian of the Launching Pad Drive-In. Wearing a space helmet and holding a rocket, this roadside giant captures the space-age optimism of the 1960s. It has become an iconic photo stop for travelers, symbolizing the whimsical spirit of Route 66.

8. Giant Jackrabbit - Joseph City, Arizona:

Joseph City, Arizona, boasts a colossal fiberglass jackrabbit that has become a playful landmark along Route 66. This oversized hare, aptly named "Jack," is a lighthearted testament to the whimsical and creative spirit found in roadside America.

Recommended itinerary for first time Tourists

Making the most of this road trip requires careful planning, especially for first-time travelers taking a Route 66 experience. With flexibility to stop and see other sites along the way, this 16- Day itinerary offers a thorough tour of the most famous destinations along Route 66. The itinerary's highlights, which cover important sites, beautiful drives, and cultural encounters en route from Chicago to Los Angeles, are listed below.

Day 1: Chicago, Illinois

Begin your journey in the vibrant city of Chicago, where Route 66 officially begins at Grant Park. Take some time to explore the city's famous landmarks, such as Millennium Park, Navy Pier, and the Art Institute of Chicago. In the evening, savor a classic

Chicago-style deep-dish pizza before gearing up for the road trip ahead.

Day 2: Chicago to Springfield, Illinois (Approximately 200 miles)

Depart from Chicago and head southwest towards Springfield, Illinois. Along the way, make a stop at the Gemini Giant in Wilmington and the historic town of Pontiac, known for its Route 66 Hall of Fame and Museum. In Springfield, visit the Abraham Lincoln Presidential Library and Museum to learn about the life and legacy of the 16th President of the United States.

Day 3: Springfield to St. Louis, Missouri (Approximately 100 miles)

Continue your journey to St. Louis, Missouri, where you can visit the iconic Gateway Arch and explore the lively downtown area. Don't miss the opportunity to sample some St. Louis-style barbecue before hitting the road again.

Day 4: St. Louis to Springfield, Missouri (Approximately 215 miles)

As you travel through Missouri, stop in the charming town of Cuba to admire its outdoor murals and quirky attractions. In Springfield, Missouri, visit the Route 66 Car Museum and explore the city's rich history as a crossroads of the Mother Road.

Day 5: Springfield to Tulsa, Oklahoma (Approximately 200 miles)

Cross into Oklahoma and make your way to Tulsa, a city known for its art deco architecture and vibrant music scene. While in Tulsa, visit the Philbrook Museum of Art and take a stroll through the historic Brady Arts District.

Day 6: Tulsa to Oklahoma City, Oklahoma (Approximately 100 miles)

Drive westward to Oklahoma City, where you can explore the National Cowboy & Western Heritage Museum and stroll along the Bricktown Entertainment District. Be sure to indulge in some delicious Oklahoma-style comfort food during your stay.

Day 7: Oklahoma City to Amarillo, Texas (Approximately 260 miles)

As you enter Texas, make a stop in Shamrock to see the iconic Conoco Tower Station. In Amarillo, visit the Cadillac Ranch, a unique art installation featuring a row of graffiti-covered Cadillacs buried nose-first in the ground.

Day 8: Amarillo to Santa Fe, New Mexico (Approximately 290 miles)

Head west into New Mexico and arrive in Santa Fe, a city renowned for its adobe architecture, art galleries, and rich cultural heritage. Explore the historic Plaza area and immerse yourself in the city's vibrant arts scene.

Day 9: Santa Fe to Gallup, New Mexico (Approximately 140 miles)

Continue your journey through New Mexico and make a stop in Gallup, a town known for its Native American art markets and Western charm. Take some time to browse the local shops and galleries showcasing traditional Navajo and Zuni crafts.

Day 10: Gallup to Holbrook, Arizona (Approximately 100 miles)

As you cross into Arizona, visit Petrified Forest National Park to marvel at its ancient petrified wood and colorful badlands. In Holbrook, don't miss the opportunity to stay in a vintage wigwam motel for a unique overnight experience.

Day 11: Holbrook to Grand Canyon National Park (Approximately 230 miles)

Embark on a side trip to Grand Canyon National Park for an unforgettable experience at one of the world's most awe-inspiring natural wonders. Spend the day exploring the South Rim and taking in the breathtaking vistas of this iconic landmark.

Day 12: Holbrook to Flagstaff, Arizona (Approximately 90 miles)

Travel westward to Flagstaff, where you can visit the Lowell Observatory and explore the city's charming downtown area. Consider taking a detour to Walnut Canyon National Monument to see ancient cliff dwellings nestled within a scenic canyon.

Day 13: Flagstaff to Kingman, Arizona (Approximately 120 miles)

Drive through scenic landscapes as you make your way to Kingman, Arizona. Along the way, consider visiting Seligman, a town known for its association with Route 66's revival and its quirky roadside attractions.

Day 14: Kingman to Oatman, Arizona (Approximately 30 miles)

Take a short detour from Kingman to visit Oatman, a historic mining town nestled in the Black Mountains. Here, you can witness wild burros roaming the streets and experience a taste of Old West nostalgia.

Day 15: Kingman to Las Vegas, Nevada (Approximately 100 miles)

Conclude your Route 66 journey with a drive from Kingman to Las Vegas, where you can revel in the glitz and glamor of the famous Las Vegas Strip. Celebrate the completion of your epic road trip with a night of entertainment and dining in this iconic desert oasis.

Day 16: Las Vegas to Los Angeles, California (Approximately 270 miles)

On your final day, drive from Las Vegas to Los Angeles as you complete your Route 66 adventure. Take some time to relax and reflect on your journey as you approach the end of this unforgettable road trip experience.

Festivals and Events

Visitors can enjoy the distinct charm and friendliness of the towns along Route 66 by attending one of the many festivals that honor the rich history and culture of the communities bordering the road along this famous route.

One of the most well-liked events along the road is the International road 66 Mother Road Festival, which begins in Springfield, Illinois. This

September three-day festival is a throwback to the heyday of American road travel, complete with vintage vehicle shows, live music, and a parade. Family-friendly events, food sellers, and craft booths all contribute to the joyous environment.

For fans of vintage cars and motorcycles, the annual Route 66 Blowout in Sapulpa, Oklahoma, is an event not to be missed. This festival features food trucks, a beer garden, live entertainment, and an automobile exhibition. Taking guided tours of nearby landmarks and exploring the historic downtown area add to the experience.

The Route 66 Summerfest is a vibrant street celebration honoring the city's relationship to the historic roadway in Albuquerque, New Mexico. Live music, food vendors, craft and art booths, and an automobile display are all available to attendees.

The region's varied heritage is highlighted through cultural performances and kid-friendly activities.

Heading west, every September Flagstaff, Arizona, organizes the Flagstaff Route 66 Days. A classic vehicle exhibition, live music, and a range of merchants offering handcrafted items and regional products are all featured at this event. The area's rich history can be learned through guided tours of iconic Route 66 locations.

One of the biggest vintage vehicle exhibits in the nation takes place in San Bernardino, California, every year during the Route 66 Rendezvous. The four-day festival includes a trip down historic Route 66, live music, and approximately 1,700 antique cars. Family-friendly events, a beer garden, and food sellers all add to the joyous atmosphere.

These festivals are but a taste of the numerous that take place along Route 66. All of them provide a singular chance to fully immerse oneself in the colorful history and culture of this famous roadway, making it an essential stop for tourists looking to have a genuine American road trip experience.

Nightlife and Entertainment

The sun setting over Route 66 signals the beginning of a vibrant nightlife scene. As twilight descends, classic diners and roadside eateries along the historic highway come to life. With retro decor, jukeboxes, and menus brimming with classic American comfort food, these establishments offer a nostalgic dining experience, inviting visitors to soak in the vintage ambiance reminiscent of the golden age of road travel.

For those seeking nocturnal rhythms, the towns along Route 66 boast vibrant music scenes. Historic venues host local bands playing blues, rockabilly, country, and folk, creating an intimate setting for live music enthusiasts.

Beyond music, Route 66's nightlife extends to cultural attractions and entertainment options. Art galleries, museums, and theaters showcase the region's rich history and heritage. Film screenings, art walks, and cultural festivals illuminate the diverse tapestry of the communities along the route.

As the night progresses, retro-themed bars and lounges pay homage to the highway's storied past. With vintage decor and specialty cocktails, these establishments provide a welcoming atmosphere for visitors to unwind after a day of exploration.

Along with unexpected roadside sites and offbeat events, Route 66's nightlife never fails to surprise. The night comes alive with a surprising charm, luring visitors to discover the quirky charm that embodies the essence of Route 66, from drive-in movie theaters to neon-lit motels.

Memorabilia and Souvenirs

The abundance of souvenirs that let visitors take a piece of Route 66's past with them enhances the experience of visiting the route. These objects are more than just baubles; they capture the essence of Route 66 and its distinct fusion of modern energy and nostalgia. The wide array of items on display at roadside stalls and boutique shops ranges from well-made handmade goods that commemorate the highway's ongoing importance to eccentric kitsch that recalls the highway's golden day. Every purchase turns the customer into a steward of Route 66's legacy by providing a concrete link to the road's rich past and present. These souvenirs, which serve as a cultural landmark, capture the spirit of the famous route and transform a routine travel experience into an enduring memory that reverberates well beyond the pavement. A rundown of some of them is presented below:

- Retro Nostalgia: Vintage-inspired t-shirts, postcards, and magnets let you relive Route 66's golden age.
- Artisanal Gems: Discover handcrafted jewelry, pottery, and artwork by local artisans, showcasing regional creativity.
- Authentic Collectibles: Antique shops offer original road signs, license plates, and gas station relics for enthusiasts.

- Quirky Cuisine: From classic diner fare to inventive snacks, savor regional delights along Route 66.
- Automotive Marvels: Immerse in vintage car memorabilia, including scale models and replicas, capturing the highway's automotive culture.
- Musical Mementos: Connect to Route 66's rhythm with souvenirs like vinyl records and retro jukebox-inspired items.
- Photographic Keepsakes: Capture the scenic beauty through photography books, prints, and framed pictures, encapsulating your journey's visual essence.
- Children's Corner: Foster adventure and cultural appreciation with Route 66-themed toys, games, and educational items.
- Literary Treasures: Immerse in written narratives, books, and poetry collections unveiling the stories embedded in Route 66.

Chapter 8: Exploring Some Top Cities Along Route 66

Overview of Chicago with Map

Chicago is the legendary starting point of Route 66, and it sits proudly in the center of Illinois. Vibrant neighborhoods, famous buildings, and a multigenerational cultural tradition are all seamlessly woven together in one city. Situated on the shores of Lake Michigan, the Windy City's breathtaking skyline demonstrates its mastery in engineering and architecture.

The unique histories of each neighborhood contribute to Chicago's eclectic identity. Investigate the history of Old Town or the artwork in Wicker Park to gain an understanding of Chicago's neighborhoods. Skyscrapers and premier theaters, museums, and galleries can be found in The Loop, Chicago's main business center.

Famous buildings like the John Hancock Center and Willis Tower serve as examples of Chicago's outstanding architectural design. These buildings, which also represent the city's ongoing architectural transition between classic and modern forms, characterize Chicago's skyline.

Chicago has a thriving environment for art, music, and food. Being the cradle of jazz and the home of the Chicago Symphony Orchestra, the city is a musical mecca. The creativity and diversity of local art are enhanced by public art projects, murals, and galleries. Foodies can embark on a gastronomic tour around the city's various neighborhoods and savor international cuisine, like deep-dish pizza and Chicago-style hot dogs.

Beyond its metropolitan attractiveness, Chicago has an abundance of parks and green areas. Millennium Park, home to the famous Cloud Gate sculpture, and Grant Park, the site of the Buckingham Fountain, provide a pleasant escape from the bustle of the city. The Lakefront Trail is a lovely route that allows locals and visitors to experience the natural splendor that surrounds the city whether they are walking, jogging, or cycling.

Overview of St. Louis with Map

Located along the banks of the Mississippi River in Missouri, St. Louis stands as a vibrant city that has played a significant role along the iconic Route 66, although it's not the starting point. While Chicago traditionally holds the title of the eastern terminus of the historic Route 66, St. Louis serves as a crucial hub along this legendary highway.

As travelers embark on their westward journey, the Gateway Arch in St. Louis welcomes them with its gleaming presence, symbolizing the spirit of adventure that defines Route 66. This iconic monument stands as a beacon, inviting road trippers to explore the cultural richness, diverse neighborhoods, and historical landmarks that characterize the city.

St. Louis's neighborhoods, from the historic charm of Soulard to the elegance of the Central West End, contribute to the city's allure, offering glimpses of its unique character. The city's cultural institutions, including the Saint Louis Art Museum, add depth to the Route 66 experience, providing an opportunity for travelers to engage with the artistic expressions that have shaped the region.

Sports enthusiasts find their fix in St. Louis, where iconic venues like Busch Stadium and the Enterprise

Center pulse with the energy of passionate fans rallying behind the Cardinals and the Blues. Culinary delights await along the way, with neighborhoods like The Hill and the Delmar Loop offering a diverse range of flavors that showcase St. Louis's gastronomic diversity.

While St. Louis may not mark the starting point of Route 66, it unquestionably stands as a pivotal city along the historic highway. Its cultural contributions, iconic landmarks, and welcoming atmosphere make it an essential stop for those seeking the authentic experience of the legendary Route 66 journey.

Overview of Oklahoma City with Map

Oklahoma City, situated at the crossroads of America, stands as a bustling destination offering a diverse range of historical sites, cultural landmarks, and vibrant neighborhoods along the renowned Route 66. Serving as a significant crossroads on the "Main Street of America," the city encapsulates the spirit of exploration associated with Route 66, extending a warm welcome to travelers initiating their westward journey.

In the heart of Oklahoma City, the revitalized Bricktown district, housed in restored warehouses, beckons with its modern ambiance, providing a contrast to the historic route. The Oklahoma City National Memorial and Museum along Route 66 add a poignant layer, commemorating the city's resilience and remembering the tragic events of 1995.

Diverse districts, such as the historic Stockyards City and the artistic Paseo Arts District, showcase Oklahoma City's varied identities. The Cowboy & Western Heritage Museum stands as a testament to the state's history and celebrates the enduring cowboy culture of the region.

For sports enthusiasts, Oklahoma City, home to the NBA club Thunder, offers a lively experience. The Chesapeake Energy Arena reverberates with the cheers of passionate fans, creating a dynamic atmosphere. Along the Route 66 corridor, local restaurants serve up delicacies like barbecue and chicken-fried steak, offering a taste of Oklahoma's culinary culture.

Nature enthusiasts can find respite in green areas like the Myriad Botanical Gardens, providing a tranquil escape within the urban landscape. The city's vibrant artistic energy is displayed on its walls through colorful murals, adding a creative touch to the overall experience.

Despite not marking the starting or finishing point of Route 66, Oklahoma City's significance along the historic highway is undeniable. Visitors are encouraged to explore, engage, and discover the spirit of this fabled American highway as the city welcomes them with its gleaming skyscrapers and nostalgic icons.

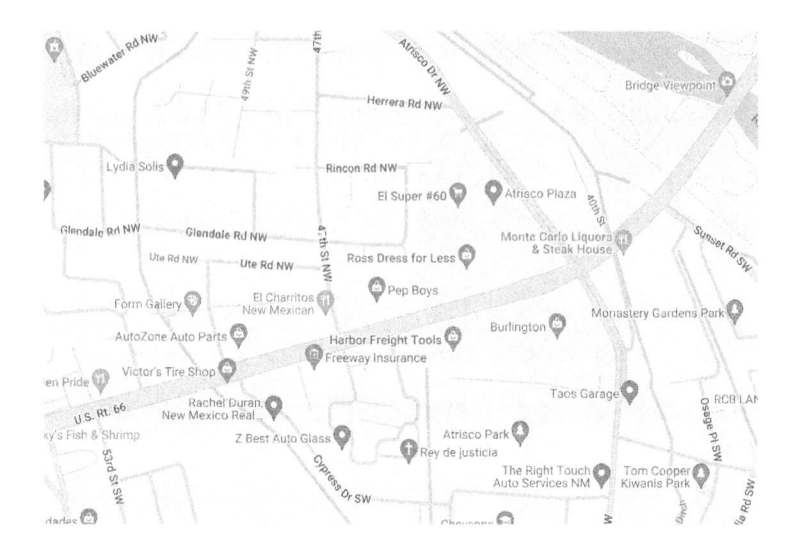

Overview of Santa Fe with Map

Santa Fe is a fascinating city that may be found in New Mexico's high desert and is accessible via the iconic Route 66. Santa Fe has a certain fascination that draws visitors to discover its vibrant art scene, rich cultural legacy, and quintessential Southwestern charm even though it's not quite on the traditional itinerary.

The center of Santa Fe is the historic Plaza, which is encircled by adobe buildings. This place features a dynamic fusion of modern and traditional design, with galleries and shops situated among centuries-old structures. The Santa Fe Trail and the ruins of a bygone period are visible to tourists as they meander through the neighborhoods.

Art is intrinsic to Santa Fe culture; the famous Canyon Road is home to a dizzying assortment of galleries featuring Native American, Hispanic, and contemporary art. The Georgia O'Keeffe Museum adds even more artistic appeal to the community by honoring the famous artist who drew inspiration from the landscapes of the area.

The varied cultural background of Santa Fe has left its mark on the food, which is a celebration of flavors. The city offers a gastronomic adventure that reflects its eclectic nature, ranging from modern takes in upmarket restaurants to classic New Mexican fare like sopaipillas and green chile stew.

The natural beauty of this city is always present because it is surrounded by the Sangre de Cristo Mountains. The city promotes visiting neighboring sites that offer insight into the area's rich past and the lives of its early residents, such as the ancient Pueblo ruins and Bandelier National Monument.

The earth tones of the adobe structures and the delicate details of their distinctive Southwestern design define Santa Fe's visual landscape. Being one of the oldest and most quaint capital cities in the country is a result of the city's dedication to maintaining its own identity.

Santa Fe entices visitors with its artistic energy, diverse culture, and beautiful surroundings even though it isn't exactly on Route 66. Santa Fe, a city that values both innovation and heritage, welcomes guests to go on an exploratory voyage where every turn reveals a new aspect of its alluring nature.

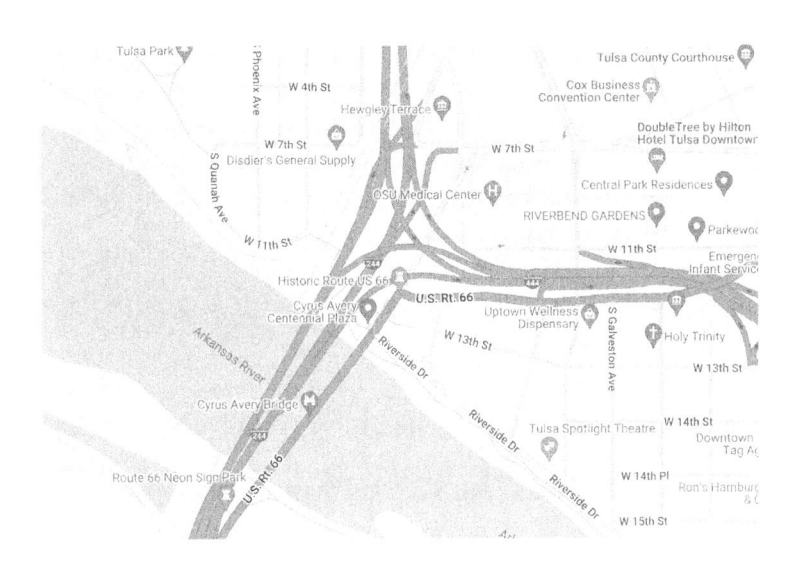

Overview of Los Angeles with Map

Los Angeles, the sprawling metropolis on the west coast, stands as a vibrant endpoint along the historic Route 66. As the final destination of the iconic "Main Street of America," Los Angeles beckons travelers with its diverse tapestry of neighborhoods, cultural landmarks, and the allure of Hollywood.

Starting from the famous Santa Monica Pier, the official western terminus of Route 66, visitors are greeted by the Pacific Ocean's expanse, symbolizing the end of their cross-country journey. Santa Monica's lively atmosphere and iconic pier create a fitting introduction to the dynamic city that lies ahead.

Los Angeles embraces its cultural diversity, evident in neighborhoods like Chinatown, Little Tokyo, and Olvera Street. The Hollywood Walk of Fame immortalizes entertainment legends, while the Getty Center showcases art against the backdrop of stunning architecture. The city's museums, theaters, and iconic landmarks contribute to its reputation as a global cultural hub.

For movie enthusiasts, Hollywood is a pilgrimage site, offering tours of celebrity homes, visits to the

TCL Chinese Theatre, and a chance to capture the iconic Hollywood Sign. The city's entertainment industry is palpable, with studios like Universal Studios Hollywood offering behind-the-scenes glimpses into the magic of filmmaking.

From the food trucks of Grand Central Market to the elegant restaurants of Beverly Hills, Los Angeles offers a plethora of culinary experiences. The city's varied culinary scene, which offers a melting pot of cuisines and gastronomic experiences, reflects the multicultural makeup of its populace.

The surrounding beaches of Venice and Malibu, as well as the vast urban oasis that is Griffith Park, are havens for nature lovers. The city offers a breathtaking backdrop for exploration because to its varied landscapes, which range from the Pacific coastline to the Santa Monica Mountains.

The route through Los Angeles captures the spirit of the American West Coast, even though the original Route 66 technically stops in Santa Monica. Travelers are left with enduring memories of their cross-country journey by the city's recognizable palm-lined boulevards, entertainment legacy, and cultural energy, which combine to create a fitting end to the historic roadway.

Overview of California with Map

California is the sun-soaked and diverse jewel on the western edge of the United States, encapsulating the final leg of the iconic Route 66 journey. As the "Golden State" beckons travelers from the vast expanses of Route 66, it unveils a tapestry of natural wonders, cultural richness, and a spirit of innovation.

Starting the California leg in the bustling city of Needles, near the Arizona border, the route winds through the Mojave Desert, revealing landscapes that have inspired countless tales of exploration and adventure. The infamous "Bagdad Café," an iconic stop along the way, serves as a testament to the resilience and creativity found amidst the arid beauty of the California desert.

Further west, the journey ventures into the historic city of Barstow, a gateway to the Mojave National

Preserve and a repository of the state's railway history at the Route 66 Mother Road Museum. Barstow, with its historic Harvey House railroad depot, stands as a living testament to California's transportation heritage.

As the road meanders towards Los Angeles, travelers encounter the picturesque town of Pasadena, renowned for its charming neighborhoods and hosting the annual Rose Bowl Parade. The sprawling cityscape of Los Angeles then unfolds, offering a dynamic blend of entertainment, culture, and culinary delights, as described in the previous passage.

Beyond Los Angeles, Route 66 extends into the heart of California, where the highway once traversed through towns like San Bernardino, known for its historic Route 66 Rendezvous, and the citrus-scented city of Riverside. The landscape transitions from urban sprawl to the coastal beauty of the Pacific, concluding at the iconic Santa Monica Pier.

California, with its diverse regions and climates, provides an unparalleled backdrop for exploration. From the rugged coastline of Big Sur to the enchanting vineyards of Napa Valley, the state offers a plethora of experiences for nature lovers and wine enthusiasts alike. The towering sequoias of Yosemite National Park and the sun-drenched beaches of San Diego further showcase the breadth of California's natural wonders.

Chapter 9: Health and Safety Precautions

Vehicle Maintenance

For a smooth and pleasurable ride, careful vehicle maintenance is necessary before setting off on a road trip along Route 66. The longevity and dependability of your car become even more important when you do a comprehensive pre-trip inspection in the middle of the gorgeous scenery.

Start by thoroughly checking all of the necessary fluids, including the power steering, coolant, brake, engine, and gearbox oils. Consistently keeping an eye on these levels is essential to your car's best performance. For optimal traction and safety, tire maintenance is equally important. Check for corrosion, wear on the tread, and inflation.

Make sure all of your lights are working properly, including the wipers, turn signals, brake lights, and headlights and taillights. With jumper cables, a tire repair kit, a flashlight, basic tools, and a first aid kit for unforeseen situations, assemble a comprehensive car emergency kit. Proactively address corrosion issues by routinely inspecting the engine oil, air filter, and battery terminals.

Plan your gas stops carefully, particularly if you live in a distant place. You should also think about having mechanics do expert inspections. Utilize adaptive driving and maintenance techniques to cope with changing weather conditions on Route 66. Give adherence to these automobile maintenance rules first priority to guarantee a dependable and roadworthy vehicle, which will contribute to a trouble-free road trip experience that highlights the beauty of the traveling experience.

Staying Safe

When taking a car journey along Route 66, one must pay close attention to their health and safety. The first step is to put together a fully functional emergency kit. Essentials including a first aid kit, flashlight, batteries, blankets, non-perishable food, and a large amount of water should be included in this package. Make sure you have all the personal hygiene supplies and prescriptions you need as well, building a complete safety net in case something unforeseen occurs.

To prevent driver tiredness, schedule regular breaks as soon as you are on the road. Due to the varied towns and cities that Route 66 passes through, it is imperative that drivers obey traffic laws and speed limits. Remain alert and informed about road closures and conditions, especially while traveling through isolated locations. This information can help you steer clear of possible problems and make the trip go more smoothly.

Give trustworthy lodging options with verified safety features first priority. Having a clean, safe place to stay when traveling makes a big difference in your general wellbeing. In light of the current COVID-19 pandemic, it is critical that you follow regulations, carry the appropriate protective equipment, and use social distancing techniques to ensure both your safety and the protection of others.

Keeping communication devices charged and providing a reliable person with your schedule improves safety in general. Keep yourself educated on the emergency services available in your area so that you can get help if you need it. You can improve your entire experience traveling the famous and historic Route 66 and guarantee fun and safety by adopting some health and safety precautions.

Emergency services

If you want to ensure your safety when driving on Route 66, you must keep your most vital emergency contacts handy. First and foremost, save the non-emergency police line for every location you visit. Never forget to dial 911 for immediate assistance in emergency or dangerous situations.

It is also important to learn about fire safety procedures and to make a note of the local fire department's contact details. In emergency situations, taking these proactive measures can make a significant difference.

In case of a medical emergency, locate nearby pharmacies, urgent care centers, and hospitals on your route. Take note of their hours of operation and contact details, especially if you are passing through more remote areas with less access to medical facilities.

Outdoor enthusiasts should be acquainted with the local search and rescue teams and keep their contact information handy when participating in outdoor activities. To remain informed about current local weather, download real-time weather apps or sign up for weather alert services.

Consider having contacts for information regarding the embassy or consulates if you're traveling from another country. To learn vital information about the places you'll be traveling through, you can also establish connections with residents or other travelers.

In case of poisoning, always have the national poison control hotline number (1-800-222-1222) close at hand for prompt aid. Lastly, provide your whole itinerary and emergency contacts to a family member or close friend. This proactive approach to emergency planning will make traveling along the historic Route 66 much safer and more secure.

Conclusion

As the sun sets on Santa Monica Pier, Jack concludes his Route 66 journey. "Route 66 Travel Guide" is more than a guide; it's a testament to the spirit of exploration. Beyond asphalt and landmarks, Jack discovers the road as a metaphor for self-discovery. The book extends an invitation to embrace the unknown, find hidden gems within, and perpetually explore life's open road.